Discovering

CENTIPEDES & MILLIPEDES

Ken Preston-Mafham

The Bookwright Press
New York · 1990

Discovering Nature

Discovering Ants
Discovering Badgers
Discovering Bats
Discovering Bees and Wasps
Discovering Beetles
Discovering Birds of Prey
Discovering Bugs
Discovering Butterflies and Moths
Discovering Centipedes and Millipedes
Discovering Crabs and Lobsters
Discovering Crickets and Grasshoppers
Discovering Damselflies and Dragonflies
Discovering Deer
Discovering Ducks, Geese and Swans
Discovering Flies
Discovering Flowering Plants

Discovering Foxes
Discovering Freshwater Fish
Discovering Frogs and Toads
Discovering Fungi
Discovering Jellyfish
Discovering Otters
Discovering Rabbits and Hares
Discovering Rats and Mice
Discovering Saltwater Fish
Discovering Sea Birds
Discovering Shrews, Moles and Voles
Discovering Slugs and Snails
Discovering Snakes and Lizards
Discovering Songbirds
Discovering Spiders
Discovering Squirrels
Discovering Trees
Discovering Weasels
Discovering Worms

First published in the
United States in 1990 by
The Bookwright Press
387 Park Avenue South
New York, NY 10016

First published in 1989 by
Wayland (Publishers) Limited
61 Western Road, Hove
East Sussex BN3 1JD, England

© Copyright 1989 Wayland (Publishers) Limited

Typeset by DP Press Ltd., Sevenoaks, Kent
Printed in Italy by G. Canale & C.S.p.A., Turin

Library of Congress Cataloging-in-Publication Data

Preston-Mafham, Ken.
  Discovering centipedes and millipedes / by K. Preston-Mafham.
      p. cm.—(Discovering nature)
  Bibliography: p.
  Includes index.
  Summary: Examines the physical characteristics, feeding, reproduction, defenses, and other activities of centipedes and millipedes.
  ISBN 0–531–18313–0
  1. Centipedes—Juvenile literature. 2. Millipedes—Juvenile literature. [1. Centipedes. 2. Millipedes.] I. Title. II. Series.   89–34787
QL449.5.P74 1990   CIP
595.6′1—dc20   AC

Contents

1
Introducing Centipedes and Millipedes

This is a giant millipede from Brazil. It has a long, shiny armored body.

What Are Centipedes and Millipedes?

Centipedes and millipedes are small animals that are related to such creatures as insects, spiders and crabs. All these animals have two very important characteristics in common – they have several pairs of jointed legs and a hard skeleton, called the **exoskeleton**, on the *outside* of their bodies. This is different from humans, who have their skeleton on the *inside* of their bodies.

Although they look similar, centipedes and millipedes are not related closely enough to be grouped together in the same scientific class of animals. The millipedes belong to the *Diplopoda* class, while their relatives, the centipedes, are placed under the *Chilopoda* class.

There are about 8,000 different species of millipedes. The smallest of

Centipedes are fatter than millipedes and have long legs and antennae.

This giant flat millipede comes from the tropical rain forests of Costa Rica.

these can barely be seen with the naked eye, because they are only 2 mm (0.08 in) long. The largest millipedes inhabit warmer parts of the world and are giants, reaching lengths of over 30 cm (12 in). These monsters can be seen roaming around in deserts, grasslands and rain forests in the **tropical** areas of Africa, Asia and South and Central America.

There are about 2,800 different kinds of centipedes. These include giant centipedes that can grow up to 26 cm (10 in) long and 2.5 cm (1 in) wide. These giant centipedes live in the tropical regions of the world.

Distant Relatives

Centipedes and millipedes could be mistaken for some of their distant relatives. Someone walking at night through a dripping wet tropical rain forest might spot a creature 7–8 cm (3 in) long with lots of pairs of thick, stumpy legs. At first glance this could be mistaken for a millipede; a closer inspection would reveal that this is a very different type of animal. Touching the creature's skin would reveal that instead of being hard and shiny like most millipedes, it is soft and velvety. It is hardly surprising that the common name for this strange animal is velvet worm, although it is no more a worm than it is a millipede.

This is a tropical velvet worm. It has lots of legs and a soft skin.

The pill bug often lives with pill millipedes under stones.

The pill millipede has a short, stout body. When disturbed, it rolls into a ball.

Velvet worms are often found in the same moist places as millipedes, under stones or bark, or inside rotten tree trunks. The body of a velvet worm does not have the many separate joints found in millipedes and centipedes, or the hard exoskeleton. Velvet worms are predators, feeding mainly on small insects such as soft-bodied termites.

If you turn over a log or stone almost anywhere, you might find another small creature, the pill bug. This is easily confused with the pill millipede. Both of these creatures are about 1.5 cm (0.6 in) long. Each has several pairs of legs and a pair of feelers, or **antennae**, on its head. When disturbed they roll up tightly into an armored ball.

What Do Millipedes Look Like?

Except for pill millipedes, all millipedes have long narrow bodies. Millipede means "a thousand legs," because they seem to have thousands of legs. In fact, even the giants never have more than about 300 legs.

A typical millipede is divided into a lot of separate segments, which make it look rather like a worm. The body is usually cylinder-shaped, although the projecting shields along the back make some millipedes look flat on top. These are actually called flat millipedes. The exoskeleton is usually hard to the touch and looks **armor-plated**. It is made of a substance called **chitin**, which is extremely light and hard; extra calcium salts in the skeleton give it greater strength. Unlike humans, a millipede does not have any bones inside its body; instead, the exoskeleton forms a

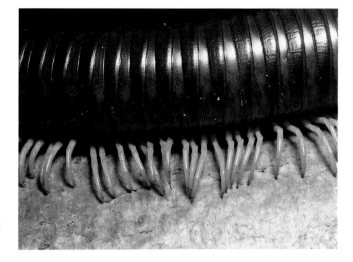

You can clearly see the body rings and jointed legs of this giant millipede.

protective case around the soft parts inside.

There is a pair of rather short antennae on a millipede's head, and on either side there is a group of tiny, simple eyes called **ocelli**. These are not as efficient as our own eyes, but as most millipedes are **nocturnal**, and find their food and each other by scent, such poor eyesight is not a serious handicap. At the bottom of the head is the mouth, equipped with jaws capable of chewing up leaves and other plant material.

Except for the first four segments and one or two at the rear end of the body, each of the segments is double and carries two pairs of jointed legs. In the males, one pair of these legs is very thick and is not used for walking; instead, it is modified into a special organ used for transferring **sperm** to the female during mating.

The eyes of these African giant millipedes are clearly visible.

A Centipede's Body

Even at a quick glance, a centipede looks quite different from a millipede. This is mainly due to the centipede's much flatter body; its legs are often long – sometimes extremely long – and they stick out on both sides.

In the larger broad-bodied centipedes, the head is large and conspicuous, jutting out in front of the body rather like a flattened plate. It carries two antennae, longer and more

This giant centipede has long antennae and legs. It lives in Texas.

thread-like than a millipede's, three pairs of jaws and groups of ocelli.

Like a millipede's body, a centipede's body is split up into a series of segments; unlike millipedes, however, centipedes usually have only one pair of legs per segment. The larger, broader kinds of centipedes have from twelve to twenty pairs of legs; the slim worm-like forms normally have well over a hundred pairs. The first pair of legs is greatly modified and acts as fangs. These are supplied with poison from special glands, and are used both for attacking **prey** and in the centipede's defense against its enemies.

A centipede's exoskeleton is softer and more pliable than a millipede's skeleton. Neither millipedes nor centipedes breathe using lungs as we do; instead, there are many tiny holes called **spiracles** along the outside of the body. These open into slim tubes

A close-up of an Australian centipede, showing its ocelli.

called **tracheae**, which allow oxygen to filter into the body by a process called **diffusion**. The spiracles of insects can be closed, but those of millipedes and centipedes are always open, putting them at risk of drying out in the sun. This is why many species are nocturnal or live only in moist, shady places.

Some centipedes are luminous, but it is not known why.

All about Legs

One of the most important ways of distinguishing millipedes from centipedes is by looking at the way they walk. Millipedes glide slowly and smoothly across the ground, almost as if their sleek shiny bodies are flowing along, rather than being carried along on a forest of short legs. This steady forward progress is achieved by waves

Millipedes spend a great deal of time carefully grooming their legs.

of movement, which flow one after the other along the rows of legs. Groups of up to twenty-two legs are involved in each of the wave-like movements, acting together on both sides of the body to carry the animal forward. Most of a millipede's legs are in contact with the ground at any one time, and only a few pairs are raised up at a particular moment. Not surprisingly, millipedes devote a lot of time to grooming their legs to keep them clean.

In contrast, a centipede's much longer legs give it a more sinuous wriggling motion. The leg movements do not occur at the same time on opposite sides of the body, but take place alternately. Sometimes, fewer than half the legs are in contact with the surface of the ground at any one time. When they are sprinting really fast, perhaps when they are fleeing from an enemy, the larger centipedes might start running into problems. Under these circumstances their long legs could start to overlap one another at each stride, resulting in dangerous tangles. This is neatly avoided by having much longer legs at the rear end of the body. These extra-lanky legs easily step past the shorter ones in front without tripping up on them. This enables the centipede to move at top speed without any problems.

This tropical giant centipede, which is 20 cm (8 in) long, can run very fast.

Centipedes Everywhere

Centipedes are far more creatures of the night than millipedes. It is rare to see a giant centipede scurrying through a tropical rain forest in broad daylight; yet that same area of forest could well be crowded with such large numbers of giant millipedes as to make it difficult to avoid crushing them underfoot.

The very flattened bodies of centipedes are perfectly shaped for sliding snugly into crevices under bits of loose bark, in old rotten logs or under rocks. When Dutch elm disease killed thousands of big old trees a few years ago, it was not unusual to find lots of the large brown common centipedes hiding beneath the peeling bark. When the bark was carefully pulled away, the centipedes dashed for cover, frantically trying to avoid the bright sunlight and retreat inside

The common centipede often slides its flat body beneath peeling bark.

any kind of dark crevice they could find. This is the natural instinct of all centipedes when faced with a sudden burst of daylight.

Certain kinds of centipedes live in the soil, a **habitat** that they share with many of the smaller, slimmer-bodied millipedes. Pale yellowish-brown thread-like centipedes with over a hundred pairs of short legs can often be dug up from garden soil where they hunt minute prey such as tiny mites. When they are on the move, their rather sinuous bodies look like millipedes.

Snake-like centipedes live in the soil and prey on tiny creatures, such as mites.

This giant millipede lives in the deserts of South Africa. It feeds in the cool evenings.

Millipedes around the World

When you dig in the garden you will often turn up a few of the millipedes that live in the soil. Apart from the giant millipedes that are often such a conspicuous sight ambling along in the tropical regions of the world, most millipedes are rather small and spend their lives hidden away beneath the bark of rotting trees or in the soil.

The tiniest millipedes are so small that they can move along underground by pushing their way between the soil particles. The slightly larger snake millipedes have to barge their way through the soil. These subterranean burrowers scarcely need eyes, which are often restricted to tiny ocelli, capable only of telling light from dark.

When the ground above is heated by the sun or frozen solid by winter frosts, the millipedes burrow their way downward to lower levels, where the soil always remains at more or less the same comfortable temperature. These soil-dwelling millipedes are generally either small or very thin, making it easier for them to make their way through the soil.

Most of the giant tropical millipedes live above ground and can even be seen trundling along in hot sunshine. Their large bodies make them less susceptible to drying out than their smaller relatives. They are sometimes as much as 30 cm (12 in) in length with over 100 segments and can be mistaken for small snakes. Such monsters are common in very dry places, even in deserts like the Kalahari in Africa. Here the giant millipedes avoid the hottest part of the day and emerge to feed only in the cool of the morning and evening or after a rainstorm.

This millipede avoids the sun altogether by living in caves.

This is one of the prettiest pill millipedes in the world. It lives in southern France.

2
Food and Feeding

This American house centipede has caught and killed a cockroach.

What Do Centipedes Eat?

In contrast to the harmless vegetarian millipedes, the centipedes feed almost exclusively on other animals. Indeed, many of the larger kinds of centipedes are ferocious hunters with long poison fangs that curve outward from just behind the head and almost meet in front of it. The **venom** is contained in a gland inside each fang, from which it flows along a narrow canal and into the prey. It is injected deep into the victim's body.

The type of prey that can be tackled depends on the kind and size of centipede and its skills as a hunter. The fast, longer-legged centipedes can manage to hunt down such agile prey as small flies. The giant centipedes of tropical regions seek out much weightier meals, preying on mice, small birds and lizards. Most centipedes, however, can manage only slow-moving, tender-bodied prey such as insect larvae, slugs, snails, worms and less ferocious centipedes.

Centipedes detect their prey mainly by using their sense of touch, which is made ultra-sensitive by means of long hairs situated on the antennae and other parts of the body, such as the legs. Once the prey has been stunned by the centipede's poison, it is speared on the projecting fangs and held firmly in place while the centipede's jaws crunch away. Only the softer parts are actually eaten; all the harder bits are thrown away.

The front pair of a centipede's legs form two curved poison fangs.

A Millipede's Diet

Almost all millipedes eat plant material only. The powerful jaws of many millipedes enable them to munch away at fallen leaves that have just begun to decay. When the leaves are in this state, chemicals, such as **tannins**, are beginning to break down, making them unacceptable as food to many kinds of animals. However, the millipede's digestion can easily cope with the leaf's contents if it is partly decayed.

This habit of chewing up large quantities of rotting leaves means that millipedes are a very important part of the vital process of returning **nutrients** to the soil in forests. The nutrients contained in the dead leaves are returned to the soil, where they will again be available for future use by the trees and other plants.

However, not all millipedes feed on

Many kinds of small, flat millipedes live among dead leaves. By eating the leaves, they help to recycle the nutrients.

plants that have died and are starting to decay. Fungi are preferred by some species; others nibble away at green plants, usually at the fine roots, which are easily attacked. Unfortunately, the tender young leaves and shoots of seedlings are also attractive to a millipede on the lookout for a meal. Millipedes are harmful pests because they attack the sugar beet crops in France and Belgium. In some parts of Kenya it is a waste of time trying to grow certain vegetables from seed, because all the tender young leaves are chewed away by the hundreds of giant millipedes that live in every garden. However, the biggest millipede in the area, a huge black beast, ignores the green plants and gnaws away at the tough bark of trees instead. Other kinds of millipedes graze on the soft coat of greenish **algae**, which is found on many tree trunks.

These tiny pink millipedes are feeding on fungi in a rain forest in Trinidad.

This giant millipede of the Mexican deserts feeds on plants at dusk.

3
Courting and Mating

A giant centipede in Madagascar wanders in search of a mate.

Finding a Mate

Centipedes are active mostly at night and it is not easy to see them while they are courting or mating. This interesting activity has, therefore, usually been watched only in captive specimens.

The male centipede has to be extremely careful when he approaches a female before mating; she is a fierce **carnivore** and might well mistake him for a tasty meal if he fails to identify himself correctly and make his purpose known to her.

Instead of taking an unnecessary risk by going straight up to her, the male bides his time and takes the precaution of making sure she knows exactly who he is. He does this by circling around and around her, tapping her gently with his antennae. If she is interested in these advances she usually responds in the same way.

This courtship circling continues until the two are ready to mate.

Unlike most other animals, male and female centipedes do not actually bring their bodies together to mate. This is because male centipedes lack a **penis**. Instead, when the male senses that the female is in a receptive mood, he spins a tiny pad of silk and places on it a little package of **sperm**. The female picks up this tiny bundle in her own sex organs, where her eggs are **fertilized** by the sperm.

Few humans have been able to watch centipedes mating. Here a female common centipede is about to pick up a sperm packet produced by the male.

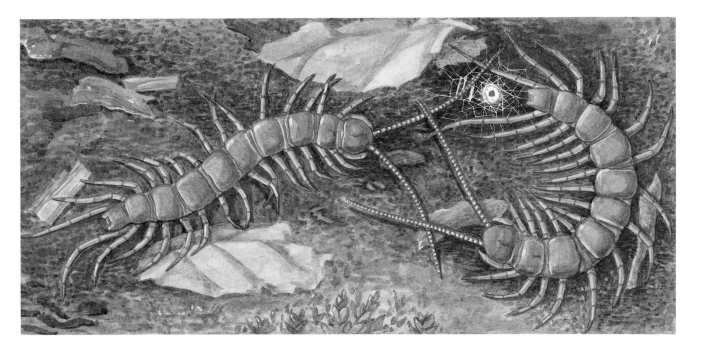

A Millipede Goes Courting

Millipedes are not as shy and elusive as centipedes, so it is much easier to watch their fascinating courtship behavior. This is especially true in the warm tropical countries of the world where giant millipedes can easily be found. Courting usually continues without interruption even when a human being is very close, for these giant millipedes are not in the least wary or fearful of humans.

A male millipede normally stimulates the female by gently caressing her with his antennae and legs. This stimulus is usually backed up by special sexual scents called **pheromones**. These enable the female to recognize a male of her own species and help her accept him as a mate. The males of some kinds of millipedes also make use of sound as part of their courtship ritual. These

This male giant millipede is gently nibbling the female's neck during their courtship.

sound signals are produced by rubbing the legs together, a process known as **stridulation**.

For some millipedes, the male's courting is made a little easier by the slight differences between himself and his partner. For example, the males of the large black and orange "Tanganyika trains" (they were named after the railroad cars in Tanganyika, now Tanzania, which are the same colors) are very smooth and polished-looking; the females have a much duller, rougher surface. This allows the male to get a better grip with his many feet while he is stretched out along her back during the courtship process, which may last many minutes. If she were shiny, too, he would be more likely to slip off.

Male millipedes have a special organ that they use to transfer sperm to the female.

Mating

The male millipede's method of persuading the female finally to accept him is to nibble delicately at her face with his mouthparts. When she becomes receptive, she turns the

These colorful giant millipedes are mating in a South African forest.

front part of her body to face him and they mate.

Unlike the male centipede, the male millipede has a special sexual organ for injecting his sperm directly into the female's body. This consists of a pair of enlarged front legs; these are normally tucked away beneath the body until the male wishes to mate. He can only do this, however, after he has first filled these special legs with his own sperm. He does this before he starts wandering in search of a mate.

Sometimes two male millipedes discover a female at the same time. This results in the strange sight of three millipedes piled one on top of the other, with the two males frantically nibbling away in an attempt to be the first to mate.

Kenyan "Tanganyika trains" often form "triple-deckers" when two males court one female.

Rearing the Young

Most female millipedes and centipedes desert their eggs after carefully laying them in a safe place, often in the soil or under rotting bark. Many millipedes first make a nest formed of soil mixed with their own droppings. However, these eggs are attacked by a variety of enemies,

Female centipedes make very good mothers. This one is curled protectively around her eggs.

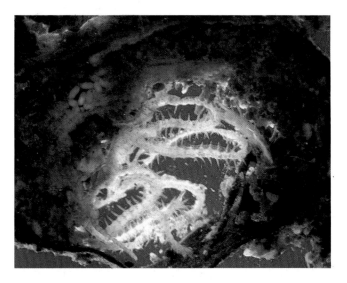

Many centipedes make small nests in which the young emerge from the eggs.

including tiny fungi, mites, insects and centipedes. It is hardly surprising then that some millipedes and centipedes stay with their eggs.

The female of one of the most common snake millipedes mixes soil particles with her own saliva and forms it into a dome-shaped nest beneath the ground. She leaves a little hole in the top through which she lays her eggs. She may make a number of these nests and stays behind in one of them to act as a guardian, coiling herself tightly around her ball of eggs.

Brooding the eggs is a common habit in centipedes. Using her head and mouthparts to remove the soil, the female digs a little chamber below ground, usually underneath a stone. After laying her eggs, she coils herself snugly around them, with her legs pointing inward. She stays in this position for long periods, only uncoiling now and then to lick one of her eggs. She probably does this to clean off **spores** of molds and fungi that would spoil them. She is brave in defense of her eggs and will try to protect them against any threat.

Millipede eggs eventually hatch into tiny larvae, which have only three

Both millipedes and centipedes go through a series of molts. This giant centipede is sitting beside the skin it has just shed.

pairs of legs. These larvae grow by **molting** their skins several times – seven times in most species. Millipedes usually live for several years, and tropical giants may reach a ripe old age of seven years or more.

In certain kinds of centipedes the larvae already have a full set of legs when they hatch from the egg. In others, the larvae have only seven pairs of legs, the rest are added at the time of molting.

4
Enemies and Friends

Most giant millipedes coil up when attacked. The head is tucked into the center of the coil, away from danger.

Armor-plated Defenses

The giant millipedes are among the armored divisions of the natural world. They bulldoze their way through even the spiniest of undergrowth, protected by their hard, slippery exoskeleton. This makes them a difficult target for many small enemies, such as ants, whose jaws cannot penetrate the millipede's tough outer surface.

Different kinds of millipedes react to danger in different ways. A giant millipede will usually try to make a run for it when disturbed, undulating over the ground on its multitude of legs at a remarkable speed. However, if it is repeatedly attacked it will give up this futile attempt to outrun its tormentor. The moment it stops, it quickly coils its body into a tight spiral. Its head is tucked away in the center – the safest possible position, where it is surrounded by dozens of spiky legs and a broad expanse of smooth armor. When coiled up like this, these giants look just like pinwheels.

The little pill millipedes so often found under stones do not even bother to make a run for it on their rather short legs. Instead, they roll up into a smooth, tight ball at the slightest hint of trouble. In this position, the head is well protected inside a close-fitting suit of armor without a single chink. After a few minutes, the millipede will poke its head out and try to escape to safety.

When confronted by an enemy, pill millipedes can roll up tightly to form a smooth, close-fitting ball without a single chink in its armor.

Chemical Defenses

Many kinds of millipedes have a second form of defense. Most millipedes have two rows of stink glands along the sides of the body. These ooze a foul-smelling and bitter liquid when the millipede is molested, perhaps by a bird. This liquid is capable of cutting short attacks by a wide variety of enemies including insects and even the fiercest kinds of ants, frogs, lizards, birds and many kinds of mammals.

When under attack many millipedes give off unpleasant-tasting chemicals. They warn predators of this by being brightly colored.

At least one kind of millipede goes a step further and is able to give off a gas capable of actually killing small creatures, such as ants, that come too close. This gas is hydrogen cyanide; it is so poisonous that we do not know how the millipede itself manages to avoid being killed by its own gas attack.

Many of these chemically-protected millipedes are also very brightly colored and patterned, especially black and orange, or black and white. Enemies such as birds soon learn to make the connection between these colors and the nasty chemicals contained in the millipedes, and leave them alone. This protective use of bright colors is called warning coloration.

Many centipedes also use chemical defenses, but the largest tropical kinds can put up a fierce fight using their huge poison fangs. These giants

A poisonous Mexican millipede walks over a pine-tree trunk. Its bright color warns predators to keep away.

sometimes bite humans. This is an extremely painful experience, but it is not likely to cause death, except possibly in very young children.

Neighbors

Millipedes and centipedes that live in soil or under bark share their habitat with worms, insect larvae, slugs and woodlice. Some of these could also provide meals for a hungry centipede. Millipedes that shelter under large stones sometimes share their accommodation with spiders, such as certain furry brown wolf spiders. This might seem dangerous, but only a few spiders have fangs capable of piercing a millipede's hard armor.

The 30-cm (12-in) giant tropical millipedes, trotting smoothly over the bark of some forest tree, are likely to be noticed by some of the more intelligent tree-living mammals, such as monkeys. Since monkeys often include meat in their diet, this could spell disaster for the millipedes, were it not for their nasty-tasting chemical defense. This is enough to put most

A red-fronted lemur sniffs inquisitively at a giant millipede, which goes on its way unharmed, protected by its bad taste.

monkeys off the idea of taking a quick bite to find out what the millipede tastes like.

The giant black millipedes that wander at night across the rust-red sands of the Kalahari Desert in Africa might also find that they have company. Sprightly little **gerbils** scamper across the sand, jumping

This hairy-footed gerbil in the Kalahari Desert has made its burrow next to the skeleton of a dead giant millipede.

nimbly over the backs of any millipedes they meet. Usually all they come across are the dead remains of their giant neighbors. When a giant millipede dies in this desert, the chitin that makes up the body segments is very resistant to decay, therefore the carcasses remain on the sand for many months. Gradually they turn white in the sun.

Animals and Insects as Enemies

Even the fiercest and most venomous of giant centipedes sometimes meets its match. On the African **savannahs** lives a large black bird with a red face, called a ground hornbill. These birds plod across the ground searching for anything edible, including large centipedes, which they pry out of their hiding places beneath bark.

Even the largest and most ferocious of centipedes are no match for swarms of tropical army ants. The fierce ants quickly overpower their victims.

The hornbill is not in danger, because its long, horny beak is immune to attack by the centipede's fangs.

Those centipedes that do not have any chemical defenses fall prey to ants, especially rampaging hordes of army ants. Dozens of these fierce little warriors will hurl themselves upon even the largest of centipedes, which is rapidly overcome and carried off by the ants.

The chemical defenses employed by many millipedes leave them with few enemies. However, in Africa the red and the grey **meerkats** will eat giant millipedes. The meerkats don't enjoy such an unsavory snack, and screw up their faces in disgust as they crunch their way through their meal.

Some kinds of assassin bugs also catch millipedes. These bugs are not put off by a nasty taste and have needle-like mouthparts capable of piercing the millipede's armor.

The African yellow mongoose will eat giant millipedes, but screws its face up in disgust as it does so.

However, catching such a slippery customer as a millipede can be a tricky task. One kind of assassin bug rubs its front legs in sticky sap oozing from trees and then uses this as glue with which it can trap even the shiniest of millipedes.

5
Learning More about Centipedes and Millipedes

In the British Isles, snake millipedes are often found grouped together under loose bark on rotting logs.

The best place to search for millipedes and centipedes is under stones or logs. However, it is important to remember that all the small creatures living in these moist, shady places depend for their very lives on having their homes replaced exactly as you found them. You should, therefore, always remember to replace the log or stone very carefully after looking underneath.

The large brown common centipedes make the best pets, but they are difficult to catch, for they sprint off extremely fast as soon as the light hits them. You can keep them in a small tank filled with earth and a layer of rotting leaves and bark. This should always be kept just moist, but not wet, for centipedes quickly dry up and die if their surroundings dry out completely. They can be fed on a varied diet of small woodlice, worms and soft-bodied insects.

Treated carefully in this way, the common centipede has been known to live for five years in captivity.

The common centipede is easy to keep in captivity and, when well looked after, should live for several years.

Glossary

Algae A group of simple plants, including seaweeds, whose most common forms on land look like a green film on tree bark.

Antennae A pair of jointed feelers on the head of a millipede, or insect.

Armor-plated Having a hard defensive covering.

Brooding Sitting on eggs in order to hatch them.

Carnivore An animal that eats meat.

Chitin A tough, horny substance from which the outer skeleton of millipedes, centipedes and insects is made.

Diffusion The way in which oxygen travels, without the help of lungs, down inside the bodies of animals such as millipedes, centipedes and insects.

Exoskeleton The hard external skeleton of animals such as millipedes, centipedes, insects and crabs.

Fertilizing The joining of a male sperm with a female egg, which eventually grows into a new being.

Gerbil A small rodent that looks like a mouse.

Habitat The place in which an animal or plant lives.

Meerkat A small African mongoose.

Molting Shedding the skin at regular intervals to allow for new growth.

Nocturnal Active at night.

Nutrients Nourishing food-material.

Ocelli Tiny, simple eyes with very limited powers of vision.

Penis The male fertilizing organ.

Pheromones Special scents produced by animals to convey messages about their sex, including willingness to mate.

Prey Animals that are killed and eaten by other animals.

Savannah A vast area of flat land with low vegetation and few trees.

Sperm The male seed that fertilizes the female egg at the start of the reproduction process.

Spiracles Tiny holes through which air enters the centipede's and millipede's body.

Spores The reproductive parts of fungi.

Stridulation A harsh sound made by rubbing together certain parts of the body.

Tannin A chemical found in many tree barks.

Tracheae Internal tubes that filter oxygen into the centipede's body.

Tropical The warm regions of the world that lie close to the Equator.

Venom Poison, often snake-poison.

Finding Out More

If you would like to find out more about millipedes and centipedes, you could read the following books:

John Burton, *The Oxford Book of Insects.* Oxford University Press, 1986

Casey Horton, *Insects.* Gloucester, 1984

Joyce Pope, *Insects.* Franklin Watts, 1985

Cover *A female giant millipede in a Kenyan forest. She is coiled up in a defensive pose.*

Frontispiece *A large millipede of the Great Smoky mountains of Tennessee.*

Picture acknowledgments

The photographs listed below were provided by Oxford Scientific Films and were taken by the following photographers: 8, 10 left (Michael Fogden), 9 left, 14, 15, 19, 21 left (J.A.L. Cooke), 9 right (Waina Cheng), 10 right (M.F. Black), 11 (Colin Milkins), 17 (Peter Parks), 18 (Barrie E. Watts), 22 (Raymond A. Mendez), 23 (George Bernard), 24, 26, 33 (Z. Leszczynski), 35 and 38 (Mark Pidgeon). All the remaining photographs are reproduced by courtesy of Premaphotos/Ken Preston-Mafham.

Index